AF131130

Albert Camus

by GERMAINE BRÉE

Columbia University Press
NEW YORK & LONDON

COLUMBIA ESSAYS ON MODERN WRITERS is a series of
critical studies of English, Continental, and other writers whose
works are of contemporary artistic and intellectual significance.

Editor: William York Tindall

Advisory Editors
Jacques Barzun   W.T.H. Jackson   Joseph A. Mazzeo   Justin O'Brien

Albert Camus is Number 1 of the series.

GERMAINE BRÉE is Professor of French Literature at
the Institute for Research in the Humanities, The University
of Wisconsin. Mme. Brée is the author of *Camus; Marcel
Proust and Deliverance from Time;* and *Gide.* She is co-
author, with Margaret Otis Guiton, of *The French Novel
from Gide to Camus* and editor of several books, including
Camus: A Collection of Critical Essays.

Copyright © 1964 Columbia University Press

First printing 1964
Second printing 1966

Library of Congress Catalog Card Number: 64-22637
Printed in the United States of America

Albert Camus

On January 4, 1960, a car heading toward Paris went out of control and crashed into a tree. Albert Camus was killed instantly. The news flashed around the world, recalling a still fairly recent day in October, 1957, when the headlines announced that the Nobel prize in literature had been awarded to Albert Camus, along with Kipling, the youngest of the Nobel laureates.

"I have turned down all engagements for 1960," Camus had written a friend. "It will be the year of my novel. I have it outlined and have started work. It will require a lot of time, but I'll get it done." In the south of France he had left the rough draft of *The First Man*, the novel that was to inaugurate a new phase in his development. He was on his way to start on another new venture, a state-subsidized experimental theater of which he had been appointed director. Camus, at forty-six, was in full possession of his powers, and he felt he could draw on what he described humorously as a "consternating vitality."

Of all the European writers of his generation, Sartre included, he was by then the man who commanded the widest attention. Not that he was universally applauded. A journalist by profession, he had found himself placed, since the years of clandestine warfare in Nazi-occupied France, at the hub of the ideological and political controversies that shook that country in the climactic mid-century period. He could hardly have avoided becoming enmeshed in the bitter argumentation of political infighting. After 1942, the year *The Stranger* came out in Paris, his meteoric fame was not calculated to inspire indulgence in the hearts of rivals he had outdistanced. Yet his critics were momentarily disarmed by his death, registering dismay in the face of a double loss—of the man himself and the work anticipated. "Whatever he did or decided in the future," wrote Sartre, "he could never have ceased to be one of the major forces in our cultural field, nor in his way could he have ceased to represent the history of France and of our century." Admirers of Camus tended to present an idealized, often a sentimentalized, image of the man; opponents tended to distort and to diminish the character, scope, and accomplishments of the complex human being he was. His contemporaries have tended to cast Camus in the role of "representative man," often reproaching him, then, with the image. Camus did not cherish the role. To "represent the history of France" or of the century had never been one of his ambitions but only to produce a literary work of intrinsic worth that truthfully reflected his own experience, and he often repeated, alone allowed him to integrate, reconcile, and discipline the violent feelings and contradictions that characterized his own passionate and basically unruly personality. His writing expressed his feelings, struggles, perplexities, and development—transmuted by the severe discipline he imposed upon himself into apparently objective literary works. That is perhaps why Albert Camus's work elicited so wide and immediate a response from far beyond the boundaries of France. A complete bibliography of articles (prepared by Robert Roeming) dealing with Camus lists some three thousand items, coming from almost every part of the world, including, in addition to the countries of Western Europe, Scandinavia, Poland, Hungary, Turkey, Israel; the United States, Puerto Rico, Mexico; the nations of South America and of Africa; Japan, Formosa, and India. According to a recent UNESCO survey his works have been translated into thirty-two foreign languages.

Camus's work has made its mark, in his own time at least, and unpredictable though the course of any literary reputation will always be, his seems to be one of the more solidly established.

Albert Camus was born in Algeria on November 7, 1913, into a family of poor, hard-working people who had settled in the village of Mondovi, near Constantine. His father's family had come from Alsace after the Franco-Prussian war, his mother's from Spain. Lucien Camus could barely read and write, his wife not at all. Drafted in 1914, Lucien was killed at the Battle of the Marne. Catherine Camus moved to a two-room apartment in the working-class section of Algiers and went to work as a cleaning woman. Camus was brought up in stringent circumstances. Five people were crowded into the apartment: a harsh grandmother, an infirm uncle, Camus's almost deaf and silent mother, and her two boys. It was to his mother that young Camus was deeply though mutely attached, and her presence haunts many of his works. Of a family that "lacked almost everything and envied almost nothing," Camus spoke with retrospective gratitude: "Merely by its silence, its reserve, its natural and restrained pride, these people, who could not even read, gave me the highest teaching . . ." Enjoying the freedom of the working-class boy, he roamed the beaches and found intense pleasure in the beauty of the Mediterranean land that compensated for the sordid brutality around him. "Poverty was never a misfortune for me," he wrote of his childhood, "for it was flooded with light." At the source of his work are the "two or three great and simple images" that awakened his sensitivity: the silent, uncomplaining mother, the light, the beauty of the earth. Not that the lad

[5]

was ingrown; he was, rather, given to violent sensuous joys and outdoor activities such as swimming and popular sports—football, and later, boxing.

Noticing the unusual potentialities of the child, a grade school teacher worked with him, preparing him to move on to high school, thence to the university. He read voraciously: first, contemporary French writers—Gide, Montherlant, Proust, and Malraux; later, the Russians—Tolstoi and Dostoevski, whom he was always to consider as his masters. Then, under the guidance of his professor, Jean Grenier, a philosopher and himself a writer, he discovered the Greeks and prepared to major in philosophy.

His working-class origin had set him apart from his fellow students. The tuberculosis he contracted at seventeen further emphasized his difference. He left home, worked in various odd jobs, mostly clerical, and continued his studies in philosophy, completing a thesis on Christian metaphysics and Neoplatonism. He made a first unhappy marriage at twenty. It lasted a year. At twenty-one he joined the Communist party, became critically restive within a year, and was excluded within three. In 1935, he launched an amateur theater group which ran for four years, presenting an eclectic program ranging from an adaptation of Aeschylus' *Prometheus Bound* to an adaptation of a recent Malraux novel, *Days of Wrath*, and including Synge, Gide, Gorki, Pushkin, Rojas . . . Camus, director, adaptor, actor, and publicity manager, was at the center of all the activity. He had an unquestionable talent for mimicry and impersonation. This is apparent in his predilection for certain techniques of literary creation: Caligula, the mad Emperor, and Jean-Baptiste Clamence, the antihero of *The Fall*, are both impersonators; and in each of Camus's three novels, the inflexions, rhythms, and modulations of a single characteristic voice are important vehicles of expression.

[6]

Camus had begun to write around 1932, and from 1935 on—as shown by the *Notebooks* he kept until his death—he was determined to become a writer. In those early years he was working simultaneously on a novel, on a play already entitled *Caligula*, and on an essay. Two slim books of essays came out in Algiers—*L'Envers et l'endroit* ("The two sides of the coin"), 1937, and *Noces* ("Nuptials"), 1938. At twenty-five, Camus belonged to a brilliant group of Algerians, proud of their Mediterranean heritage, who intended to put North Africa on the literary map. But his celebrity was still strictly local.

The year 1938 was a crucial one. He had intended to become a professor, but he could not pass the medical examination required by the government. He then turned to journalism, writing for a liberal left-wing paper, *Alger Républicain*. Reporting on scandalous instances of the miscarriage of justice, then on the desperate plight of the Berber peasants in Kabylia, Camus began to show unsuspected strengths.

Literature, philosophy, theater, journalism, a deep concern with social justice—by 1938 the main lines of Camus's activity and interests were established. With the outbreak of World War II events beyond his control were to project him out of Algeria and on to the European scene. Reformed for reasons of health, his paper suppressed by the Algerian authorities because of its openly pro-Arab sentiments, and he himself requested to leave, Camus moved to Paris in March, 1940, to work on the staff of the daily *Paris-Soir*. He married again in Lyons in December, 1940, returning to Oran in January, 1941. From that time until the fall of 1943, when his activity in the clandestine underground network "Combat" can be traced, Camus's movements are hard to follow. In the spring of 1942 he was in France. He seems at that time already to have become involved in some clandestine activity that took him to Saint-Étienne and Lyons. Meanwhile, the publication

[7]

in Paris of *The Stranger* (1942) and *The Myth of Sisyphus* (1943) brought him immediate recognition. He left for Paris in the spring of 1943 to work as reader for the publishing firm of Gallimard. In the fall of that year, under the name of Bauchart, he assumed responsibility for the publication and diffusion of the newsheet *Combat*, organ of the network of the same name, a dangerous task. Camus also went under the name of Albert Mahé. He narrowly escaped from the Gestapo when arrested while carrying a layout for an issue of *Combat*. When, with the liberation of Paris in August 24, 1944, *Combat* came out in the open, Camus, at thirty-one, enjoyed a double fame. He was awarded the Medal of the Liberation, a rare honor.

From 1944 on, Camus's public life reflects the agitations and the almost unbearable disappointments that followed the Liberation. After 1954 the savage Algerian conflict that he had predicted tore at his heart. Of the hundreds of editorials and articles he wrote, only a few are available in English. They present a chronicle of the swiftly changing atmosphere, the startling events of those years. They show the evolution of a thought that was to lead, in 1951, to the publication of *The Rebel*, an essay that sparked a bitter controversy and consecrated the rift that had been growing between Sartre and Camus. Four plays, produced with varying success—*The Misunderstanding* (1944), *Caligula* (1945), *State of Siege* (1948), and *The Just Assassins* (1949)—had been accompanied by a long novel, *The Plague* (1947). *The Rebel* marked a new point of departure, which *The Fall* (1956) emphasized. New themes and new techniques now characterized a volume of short stories, *Exile and the Kingdom* (1957). Once again Camus became involved with the stage, adapting and directing a half dozen plays, two with success—Faulkner's *Requiem for a Nun* (1956) and Dostoevski's *Possessed* (1959). A new block of work was in preparation—*Don Juan*, a play and an essay, and *The First Man*.

A merely factual account of Camus's life leaves out the essential. Camus belonged to a generation deeply affected by historical circumstances. He recalled in his Stockholm speech those "more than twenty years of absolutely insane history," when he felt "lost hopelessly like all those of [his] age in the convulsions of the epoch . . ." He was twenty when Hitler came to power in the politically agitated thirties. He saw the rise of several great totalitarian states, the collapse of the socialist and liberal movements in Europe, the purges in Russia, police terrorism and torture spreading over Europe, total war, concentration camps. The Algerian conflict was at its height when he died. It was not an era calculated to inspire serenity. Besides the toll in time, energy, and health, Camus felt that the times had also imposed on his work an orientation it might not otherwise have had.

Like many young intellectuals—even more than most perhaps, because he came from an inarticulate proletarian group— he felt the need to rethink the world, to make sense of what, with millions of others, he was witnessing and experiencing. The ideas he developed in his essays, the themes that patterned his work were not abstract exercises in theoretical logic or literary games. He was accustomed to harsh realities and with these he grappled intellectually, convinced that thought must be welded to action, that there are more fundamental elements involved in human conduct than the niceties of theoretical, verbal argumentation.

Brutal as they were, the years between the two world wars in France were rich in artistic achievement and intellectual ferment. There were indeed "two sides to the coin": a sense of doom, but also a restless, exciting sense of a new world in the making. Both were reflected in the arts and in the violence of the ideological conflicts that kept the French outside totalitarianism but took them instead to the brink of civil war. Algeria was on the periphery of all the agitation, more stable in appearance, gayer, more confident of the future. In his first essays, with a keen eye for the shortcomings of his compatriots and a humor all the freer because directed at himself as well, Camus described typical North African attitudes—the elementary ethics, the reliance on immediate uncomplicated physical satisfactions in a land that lavishly proffered them, the religious and metaphysical void, a mute accord with the natural elements and the beauty of the Mediterranean homeland, and an equally mute horror of death. A people, he noted, gay and resigned, without traditions, "without questions." It was Camus's illness that seemed to have awakened his mind to questions he might otherwise have ignored. He explored the many avenues of secular philosophy, the Greeks, the philosophers of history—Hegel, Marx, and Spengler—the existential and phenomenological thinkers rapidly replacing Kant in the minds of the young: Kierkegaard, Nietzsche, Shestov, Husserl, Jaspers, Heidegger.

But, unlike some of his brilliant French predecessors and contemporaries, Gabriel Marcel, Merleau-Ponty, Jean-Paul Sartre, and Simone de Beauvoir, Camus did not think of himself as a professional philosopher. He was not interested in building a coherent, philosophical explanation of man's situation in the world. In fact, he had a rational aversion toward all such systems. Perhaps because of his background he was much more interested in becoming, in a Socratic sense, a man with an ethic. It was on ethical grounds that he had rejected a Marxist ideology which in the Stalin-dominated thirties was, he felt, merely a façade cynically masking political opportunism and the repressive mechanisms of a police state. What he diagnosed as the single greatest development of his time was the widespread existence of a fundamental nihilism, whether latent or carefully reasoned. The intellectual skepticism born of political experience and philosophical eclecticism; the onslaught against the various forms of rationalism inherited from the Enlightenment; Nietzsche's attacks on Western values; Spengler's prophecies of doom grafted on prevalent notions concerning the predetermined course of history—these merely gave that nihilism its arguments.

With literature, Camus was thoroughly at home. His early book reviews in *Alger Républicain*, two of them of Sartre's first fictional works; the critical essays he wrote throughout his career, the two earliest of which (on Dostoevski and Kafka) he later included in *The Myth of Sisyphus;* and the notes he jotted down and the prefaces he wrote—all give a fair account of his tastes. He shared the predilection of his generation for Dostoevski and Kafka, Melville, Faulkner, and Hemingway. But he also made his own choice among the "greats" in literature, a classical choice—the Greeks, Shakespeare, and the French classics. Of the brilliant group of French writers during the twenties and thirties, three gained his sympathetic attention: Montherlant, whose haughty isolation and aristocratic ethics he admired; Giono, whose love of the elemental beauty of the world he shared; Malraux, whose tense and dramatic investigation of modern man's "fate," as it was being molded in the great revolutionary movements of the Far East, raised questions that echoed in Camus's own mind. But to no one of the moderns did he give his full allegiance.

In these prewar years, still bathed for him in Mediterranean light and vibrant with energy, Camus wrote his first series of works. A novel, *The Stranger;* a play, *Caligula;* an essay, *The Myth of Sisyphus* developed almost simultaneously. In his *Notebooks* he later grouped them together under a single

[11]

label—Sisyphus: Cycle of the Absurd. A fourth work, belonging to the same group, *The Misunderstanding*, was in an embryonic stage in 1939. It serves as a kind of transition to the works that form Camus's second group.

Although not systematically adhered to—the lyrical essays collected in *Summer* and the short stories of *Exile and the Kingdom* seem unrelated to any preconceived design—the pattern of this first series was maintained by Camus. In the postwar years he produced a novel, *The Plague;* two plays, *The Just Assassins* and *State of Siege;* and an essay, *The Rebel.* Again he grouped them under a single label—Prometheus: Cycle of Revolt. His *Notebooks* show that he had projected further developments: a cycle of Nemesis, or measure; a cycle dealing with love or compassion. In each case he projected a novel, plays, an essay. To a question that concerned the relationship of his essays to his novels, Camus answered:

I write on different levels precisely to avoid mixing genres. So I wrote plays in the language of action, essays in a rational form, novels about the heart's obscurity. True these different kinds of books say the same thing. But, after all, they were written by the same author and, together, they form a single work.

A single work, a single author, but the "cycles" of Camus's work reflect in turn different atmospheres: prewar Algiers, with its predictable routines and enjoyments; the tense dreary days of occupation with their regimentation and dull horror; the intellectual confusion and frustrated political idealism of the fifties; the slow return to the rhythm and concerns of private living. Camus seems to have been exceptionally sensitive to the complex emotional, political, and intellectual currents of his time.

Readers of *The Stranger* are always tempted to identify Camus with the hero of his novel, Meursault. Yet the first two volumes Camus published show the fallacy of such an identification. The five essays in *L'Envers et l'endroit*—"Irony," "Between Yes and No," "Death in the Soul," "Love of Life," and "The Two Sides of the Coin"—combine brief vignettes of the Algerian working-class milieu, with an orchestration of two fundamental and contradictory themes: the "nothingness" that lies at the heart of human life and the glory of that life itself. *Noces* with lyrical eloquence develops the two themes— of life, of death—against the background of the Mediterranean landscape: the glory of life in "the morning sun" of Tipasa, and the "great joy" filling the vast space of sky and sea; the certainty of death voiced by the "arid splendor" of the dead city of Djémila; life, savored on the burning Algerian beaches in the heart of summer; the reconciliation with death glimpsed among the gentle hills of Italy. In no immediate sense was young Camus a stranger among men or to this earth. "I am happy, on this earth," he wrote in his *Notebooks*, "for my kingdom is of this earth." And Patrice, his first fictional hero, reiterates: "I shall speak of nothing but my love of life."

It has become customary, when discussing *The Stranger*, to see the story, not as fiction but as an abstract philosophy of the "absurd." Camus perhaps is partly responsible for the mis-understanding, having himself launched the term. But the preface to the *Myth of Sisyphus* expressly states that a philoso-phy of the absurd is precisely what we lack, and it was not Camus's intent to furnish that philosophy. Through the *Note-books* we can follow the adventures the novel underwent be-tween 1935 and May, 1940, when it was finished.

Camus had envisaged a quite different book, *La Vie heureuse* ("A happy life") a semiautobiographical novel, pre-sented through a third-person hero, a would-be writer, Patrice Mersault. Camus wrote a first and then a second version, in the course of which the title shifted to *La Mort heureuse* ("A happy death"). As he worked, certain themes of *The Stranger*

[13]

appeared, sometimes separately, sometimes connected with the story but lost in a maze of other themes. *The Stranger* took shape slowly, through trial and error, the result of a long circuitous search. The book that emerged was strikingly different from the one Camus had planned.

The story of *The Stranger* is uncomplicated, on the surface at least. Meursault, an office clerk in Algiers, receives a telegram announcing the death of his mother in an old people's home. He asks for a two-day leave, attends the funeral, and then comes back to Algiers. He goes to the beach, picks up a nice girl, Marie, and takes her to the movies. They then go to his apartment and make love. By chance he becomes involved in the unsavory affairs of a neighbor, Raymond, a pimp who starts a dangerous feud with some Arabs. One Sunday, Raymond, Meursault, and Marie go off together for an outing. The Arabs follow them. Raymond gets into a fight. Later, Meursault, who prudently had taken Raymond's revolver, encounters one of the Arabs. A knife flashes in the sun, Meursault pulls the trigger . . . He is arrested, tried, and condemned to death.

Although Camus's first novel had little in common with *The Stranger*, two of its themes point to the two centers of tension in the novel: a mother-son estrangement and a man sentenced to death. It is only little by little that the estranged son became the man sentenced to death and that Camus provided him with an act—a murder—justifying the sentence. Whatever interpretations *The Stranger* may suggest, and they are many, one should not forget that his novels, as Camus said, speak of the "obscurity" of the human heart. It was the voice of the man sentenced to death that spoke first, though not alone, in the heart of a young man who as an adolescent had almost died in complete solitude, faced with the "surprising indifference" of the world, an indifference which seems to have long echoed in his own empty heart. Meursault's fundamental trait, his indifference, seems to be, in part at least, a reflection of that initial experience; hence the power this singular hero derived over his creator's imagination.

"Today mother died, or perhaps yesterday . . ." So begins the novel. Camus, after much experimentation, adopted for *The Stranger* a form of the widely used first-person narrative. Meursault tells his own story as it evolves. Attempts have been made to discover a definite point in time from which Meursault views the events he recalls, but they have all been unsuccessful. Questionable if discussed on realistic grounds, the device was obviously chosen for aesthetic reasons, and proved to be remarkably persuasive. Because of the shifting perspective of his story, the controlling point of view is not entirely Meursault's. He is unaware of the future ramifications of his acts, himself advancing blindly toward a trap carefully laid for him by the circumstances he notes. His position is curiously analogous to what happens in a dream, where the dreamer both evolves the dream and lives in it; yet unlike the nightmarish world of Kafka, the world of Meursault is a brilliantly lighted, clearly delineated, everyday world, that of Algiers.

The narrative device chosen by Camus has advantages: the persuasive immediacy of the situations described, the creation of a climate of chance, suspense, and yet inevitability, and for Camus the freedom to create sharp fluctuations in the reader's emotional reaction to Meursault. The first pages are in a low-keyed, matter-of-fact tone, and the reader views the funeral, the old people's home and its inhabitants through Meursault's eyes. But as Meursault proceeds, telling of his return, his involvement with Marie and then with Raymond, the reader becomes alarmed. He finds himself obliged to view and judge from the outside, even though he is entirely dependent upon Meursault for the facts and atmosphere of the story itself. A first distancing is created, but strictly within the confines of Meursault's self-contained world. The novel ends in uncertainty, so far as Meursault's immediate fate is concerned. The appeal on his behalf submitted by his lawyer has not been acted upon, a loophole is left. The voice of Meursault therefore is the voice of a living man, a man sentenced to death to be sure, but one who, within the limits of the novel, unlike us, will never die. Begun as the most ordinary of anecdotes concerning the most indistinguishable of men, the novel has thus moved toward myth. Set apart from all men because he killed a man, judged and condemned to the guillotine, Meursault, speaking to us as a "man-sentenced-to-death" exemplifies the most universally shared human situation that exists. Thence, no doubt, the enigmatic quality of the character.

The story falls into two parts: the account of the events that lead Meursault from his mother's funeral to the murder on the beach; the events that concern Meursault's imprisonment and trial and stop just short of his execution. Factual in appearance, the first part describes an ordinary routine life, lived among ordinary people, carrying with it a flavor of sun and sea, the sense of a direct semiconscious, nonverbalized enjoyment of simple physical things—swimming, sunshine, the softness and charm of a young girl's presence. The second part of the story brings no new events, only a judgment. It takes place indoors—whether prison or courthouse—and in solitude, whether actual solitude or, as during the trial, moral solitude. But the young man, who in the opening pages of the book had asked his boss for leave to attend his mother's funeral, has traveled a long way by the time he reaches the end of his tale.

Behind Meursault there is, of course, Camus, the novelist, who controls both Meursault's changing experience and the reader's reactions, invisibly manipulating a situation that seems to move inexorably of its own momentum. He can thus charge it indirectly with a dramatic irony that is not always apparent at the first reading. It underlies the focal situation—murder, however unintentional—and the focal problem: the relation of Meursault to his act. The events that lead to Meursault's fatal encounter with the Arab on the beach are set up with great care. Originally, they do not concern Meursault at all. The Arabs' anger is directed at Raymond, Meursault's neighbor, for his blatantly brutal treatment of his Arab mistress. Meursault is involved only indirectly, by association. Even the revolver he holds at the time of shooting is not his. He had taken it from Raymond as a precaution against violence. When he pulls the trigger, in the heat of the midday sun, his gesture is irrational, unforeseen, unmotivated.

Implicated in a quarrel not his own, driven by the violent pressure of outer elemental circumstances—the pitiless glare and heat of the sun—a man has killed another man. There is no going back on the act. Excluding all ordinary "psychological" motivations for the crime, Camus carefully designed Meursault's situation so that the mechanisms of chance and outer pressure would lead to this brief loss of control.

Meursault is obviously not a "criminal" type. There is little to distinguish him except his tendency to say nothing and a kind of passive gentleness: he is friendly, sympathetic to others, apparently content with a life he sees no reason to change. He is scrupulous in the expression of his feelings, but seemingly far more indifferent with regard to his acts. He likes to make love to Marie, but he will not say he loves her. Yet he acquiesces when she suggests marriage. He acquiesces too when Raymond involves him in his plan of vengeance, thereby underwriting Raymond's primitive ethical code. Behind the character's apparently disconnected acts one begins to see a constant; Meursault is a man who acquiesces in what is. His

[17]

inertia leads to the irrevocable last acquiescence, the finger on the trigger, and the forcible transformation of his life.

At no time does Meursault plead innocence; nor does Camus at any time suggest that he is innocent. That, with the shooting, something has gone irrevocably wrong, Meursault knows immediately, though neither what nor why. The murder committed, we move away from the deceptively realistic tone of the narrative, toward a far more stylized treatment of Meursault's situation.

The second part of the novel is concerned with the enigmatic problem of Meursault's act, a problem as puzzling to Meursault as to the reader. Of the usual interpretations, Camus makes short shrift, presenting them ironically in Meursault's semiburlesque interviews with the prosecutor, magistrate, and lawyer, and in his account of his trial. The first-person narrative now establishes a strange dissociation between the facts and feelings Meursault had previously described, and the attempts made by others to interpret these coherently. A definite shift in perspective is introduced: the reader finds himself in the position of judge, jury, and privileged witness. He and Meursault alone know the facts. Camus has thereby put upon him the burden of an explanation Meursault is unable to furnish. Self-critical and self-correcting, the novel rapidly moves toward its end.

The official characters Meursault encounters during his imprisonment and trial are little more than subtly wrought masks incarnating and deliberately satirizing interpretations that Camus rejects as irrelevant—guilt, remorse, atonement, conversion. The trial itself, seen from the outside, is little more than a grotesque preview of the many possible arguments for or against Meursault, his character, and motivations. They leave Meursault intact and the problem of his act unsolved. Meanwhile in his prison Meursault awakens to a new dimension of

[18]

life, an inner awareness that he had totally lacked. The death sentence, after an initial shock, finally sets him on the path of an epiphany that reaches back to the beginning of the novel, wrenches Meursault out of his passive state, and prepares him to counter the terror of death with the concentration of all the forces of life. His apparent indifference to his mother's death, to Marie's love, drops from him like a cloak as he confronts the chaplain who comes to speak to him of compensation in an afterlife. In the solitude of his prison what Meursault reaches for goes deeper than guilt and remorse. He had acquiesced to the "natural death" of his mother, indifferent to the rituals with which society surrounded it; he had himself participated in the death of another human being, indifferent to the interpretations society put upon his act. The awakening that follows his death sentence alone can bring into focus those two moments unifying the pattern of his experience. Meursault sees, at last, that to exist is happiness. His indifference to the sights and smells of the world turns into a conscious love; his passive acquiescence to the violence done human beings turns into a passionate revolt against death and a sense of human fraternity. He can now understand the small joys that filled the last days of his mother's humble life. The revolver shot that precipitated him from his semiconscious existence into the closed universe of his mind has, as its counterpart, the violent act of consciousness whereby Meursault emerges from his isolation assuming his identity as a human being, the full responsibility for his life in its beauty and incomprehensible strangeness. Camus leaves Meursault on the threshold of a new awareness and a new passion, suspended between life and death. But this does not account for the two most dramatic passages in the book—the murder itself and Meursault's last imaginary bid for the hatred of the crowd, should his execution take place.

Twelve years after the publication of *The Stranger*, Camus wrote a semi-ironic and typically paradoxical preface which has been widely quoted, often without a glint of humor and out of context. "From my point of view," he remarked,

Meursault is not a human wreck, but a poor and naked man, in love with the sun that leaves no shadows. Far from lacking sensitivity, he is animated by an intense, because stubborn passion, a passion for the absolute and for truth. It is still a negative truth, the truth of being and feeling, but without it, there can be no conquest of oneself or of the world.

This then would be the unexpressed inner compulsion that drives Meursault. The refusal to conclude without evidence, to rely on words, to go beyond what he thinks is true, to strike attitudes, to "plead innocent" or "plead guilty." In Camus's eyes this makes of him a man who, in a sense, accepts death for the sake of truth. "I have sometimes said and still paradoxically," Camus concludes, "that in the person of my character I had tried to create the only Christ we deserve," a challenging statement.

However we wish to interpret the novel, it is clear that we cannot be satisfied to read it merely as a story. Camus obviously intended to create an autonomous, exemplary figure. At one time in his *Notebooks* he had envisaged a novel centering on a character conceived as "L'Indifférent" ("The indifferent man"). Meursault's shattering adventure has its source in characteristic indifference, and its significance seems to lie in the revelation of the basic and dangerous inadequacy of this attitude. It leads him into a trap where its initially imperceptible inadequacies are fully revealed and then, in a reverse movement, transcended. This dialectical method of creation is typical of Camus's writing, and reminiscent of André Gide, but in Camus's case it would seem more obviously connected with Plato.

[20]

When *Caligula*, a four-act play, was produced on the Paris stage in 1945, it was an indubitable success, the greatest that, as playwright, Camus was ever to enjoy. For each new production of his play—in 1950, 1957, and 1958—he reworked his text, modifying it quite considerably. But by and large it remained the play Camus had written in his twenty-fifth year, Caligula's age in the first version of the play.

If, of the twelve ferocious emperors described by Suetonius, it was Caligula who caught Camus's fancy, this was no doubt because of that emperor's youth and of the peculiar forms his madness took. Camus provided a motivation that transformed the emperor from a historic into a contemporary, though imaginary, figure. Camus, in those years, was preoccupied with death. The "man-sentenced-to-death"—his double in a sense—had appeared in the *Notebooks* approximately a year before. At the root of Caligula's adventure is an emotional and intellectual confrontation with the finality and inevitability of death.

The first act of the play sets the stage for the developments that take place in the subsequent acts, three years later. Its purpose is to establish the inner climate of distress that gives their coherence to Caligula's fantastic external acts and to set up the outer circumstances that give these acts their dramatic plausibility. Caligula, a "relatively attractive prince," has been absent for three days, since the death of Drusilla, his beloved sister and mistress. The curtain rises, just before his return, on a group of more or less anxious patricians. Four people in the emperor's entourage stand out: Caesonia, his mistress; Cherea, an older, thoughtful, and reserved man; Scipio, a young poet; and Helicon, a former slave freed by Caligula, and his henchman. They sound the note of concern that prepares Caligula's intensely dramatic entry. Distraught, and like Hamlet, proffering strange and incongruous words, Caligula spreads consternation around him. Camus attempts to reveal the emperor's state of mind through gestures and acts, and by words that emanate from it but do not explicate it. Violently striking a gong to alert the palace, Caligula effaces from a mirror the image of the "relatively attractive prince," thus announcing the advent of a new Caligula. It is clear to the audience that Caligula's "descent into hell" has sent him back transformed.

When the curtain rises on the second act, three years have gone by and Caligula has become an "impossible" character, a monster, a ferocious tyrant, isolated in his court, attended only by Caesonia and Helicon. Reluctantly, his former friends, Scipio and Cherea, have been forced to abandon him. As a revolt gains momentum, Caligula accumulates grimly burlesque masquerades that mock, humiliate, kill, and devastate. In a last powerful scene, completely isolated now, Caligula breaks the mirror, confronts his assassins in whose plot he has deliberately acquiesced and dies with a last wild cry: "I am still alive."

Brilliant in conception, and richly executed in a vibrant, lyrical language that moves with ease from irony, to pathos, to tragic intensity, the play has, nevertheless, certain weaknesses. The first act raises the question of the connection between Caligula's confrontation with death and the crisis heralded by the strokes on the gong. The suspense it creates should be slowly resolved in the successive acts. But the young dramatist has eluded the problem. The three-year lapse he allowed himself between Act I and Act II does not bring about a transformation in depth of character or situation. In the next stage, the inner coherence of the play is somewhat sacrificed to the spectacular masquerades that seem to have tempted the stage director in Camus; their arbitrariness detracts from their plausibility. The significance of the main character is overshadowed by the horrifying stage business that accompanies Caligula's

ferocious appearances. The primary theme of the play, Caligula's self-destruction, is obscured.

Caligula's inner development, suggested in the first act, has
its source in his discovery of a simple yet startling truism:
"Men die, and they are not happy." Hence his violent revolt,
his intolerable sense that all life is a futile masquerade, his need,
as a compensation, to achieve something "impossible"—change
the world, possess the moon, reverse the seasons, conquer
death itself, assert his absolute freedom. Concomitantly he
wants to spread his gospel and communicate his own stark
revelation. All-powerful, he decides to impersonate cold fate.
Logical to an extreme, he consistently identifies himself with
the arbitrary, derisive, or cruel forces that destroy human se-
curity. But in the course of this identification, of necessity he
destroys his human self. His murder, accepted by him, is a
"superior suicide," brought about by the tragic realization that
he has miserably failed. *Caligula*, as Camus conceived it, "is the
story of the most human and tragic of errors," an error whose
nature Caligula recognizes just before he dies: "My freedom
was not of the right kind."

A tragic human error, implacably carried to its logical limit,
is also at the dynamic core of *The Misunderstanding*, a three-
act play produced a year before *Caligula*, but written several
years later. The play reaches back in setting and mood to 1936,
to a dismal night of solitude Camus had spent in Prague. Written in the atmosphere of occupation, "in the middle of a country encircled and occupied," it became heavily charged with
a gloom and "claustrophobia" entirely new in Camus's work.
The story of *The Misunderstanding* is a variant of an old folk-
loric tale whose components are simple: an isolated inn and an
innkeeper who assassinates travelers in order to rob them. The
variations on the pattern are innumerable and its symbolic potentialities are evident. Camus tightened the plot so as to create,

[23]

he said, an "impossible situation." The inn, situated in the heart of Czechoslovakia, is run by two women, an old mother and her daughter, Martha. When the curtain rises, they are discussing the arrival of a traveler, whom they are to drug and drown in the weir that night, like others before him. But with a difference. He is to be the last, for their ultimate purpose will now be achieved. They will have the money that will bring them freedom and allow Martha at last to reach the sunny beaches of the South. The traveler appears and the trap closes. He reveals—but only to the audience—both his purpose and his identity. A prodigal son, who left home twenty years before, now a wealthy man living in the warm Southern land to which Martha aspires, he has come to help his mother and sister. But he plans to remain incognito until he is recognized. The play moves grimly to its end—in a kind of nightmarish tug of war between the inflexible mechanism of murder, set off by the traveler's arrival, and the repressed emotions and hesitations of mother, daughter, and son fumbling toward its arrest. Jan, the son, will be recognized, but only after he has been killed. His mother will join him in the weir. Martha, his sister, commits suicide, but only after she sees and denounces the horror of the trap into which she has fallen. Maria, Jan's wife, is left in moral torture to face the bitter uselessness of it all. Her anguished cry for help elicits from the old, enigmatic, and in appearance, mute, waiter who haunts the inn, only a single syllable: No. "A son who expects to be recognized without having to declare his name and who is killed by his mother and sister as a result of the misunderstanding—this is the subject of the play." The whole design of the plot points to an underlying, hidden meaning.

Camus admittedly was interested only in one form of drama —tragedy. In this he was not alone. Eugene O'Neill in America; T. S. Eliot in England; Giraudoux, Anouilh, and Montherlant in France, to mention only a few names, all experimented in that form. One of the more tempting paths Camus's predecessors had explored was the reinterpretation in modern terms of well-known Greek themes. In his own experiments as dramatist, Camus seems to have deliberately attempted to free his plays from dependency on the ready-made tragic characters and conflicts so often reinterpreted by contemporaries. He wanted to find a "modern" design that could disclose the particular forms the tragic conflict assumes at the present time.

In its structure, *The Misunderstanding* harks back to the Greeks: the rigid masklike quality of the two women, the fatal chain of crime engendering crime, the murder within the family group, the inflexible working out of an initial purpose, and the recognition theme. *Caligula* is more closely related to the Molière technique of unleashing a Tartuffe or Don Juan to wreak havoc within a relatively "normal" world. But the nature of the havoc wrought is different and at first eludes the mind. Camus's idea of the "tragic conflict," partly derived from Nietzsche, he also outlined: the coexistence of two equally necessary, equally valid but irreconcilable principles or orders that place individuals in "impossible," hence incomprehensible, situations where the irrational prevails. He thus conceived his theater as a "theater of the impossible," presenting in Caligula an "impossible character," and in *The Misunderstanding* an "impossible situation." The restless, impatient surge of human beings to transcend their limitations seemed to him the very essence of the modern tragic situation.

The "impossible" figuration on stage therefore has a significance beyond itself, not explicated by the characters. The spectator or reader must make his way back to the initial feeling and thought that animates the play. Camus's purpose is to awaken the consciousness—rather than, like Hamlet's, to "catch the conscience"—of his audience.

[25]

For *Caligula* the pattern, though somewhat obscured, is clear: Caligula's initial revolt is thoroughly human, involving a sense of the poignancy of living. He cannot accept the haphazard game nature plays with human life. Since he cannot attach the metaphysical, social, political ordering of human existence to a universal frame of reference, he sees it as a derisory sham. He embodies thereby a tragic conflict: his revolt negates his logical conclusions. This "impossible" position is mirrored in his passionate desire to impose his vision on all about him, while using a method that makes communication impossible. It is mirrored too in a sense of moral freedom that leads him only to the dead end of despair. If Caligula embodies one of the latent tendencies of our thinking, it is from Caligula that the play wants to free us.

The Misunderstanding is more obscure. Martha and her brother are committed to the same very human project: to transform the bleak situation at the inn, to achieve happiness. Jan, secure in his own happiness and love, vaguely takes for granted a situation where things "work out," a natural order in which a mother will always recognize her son; he walks confidently into the mechanical, abstract pattern of crime set up in the inn by Martha, whose "right" to achieve happiness justifies the means automatically employed. The two approaches, inflexibly pursued by brother and sister, each with the same goal in view, blind them to the recognition of their real situation: the brother and son is not recognized; he does not even glimpse the nature of the situation he came to remedy. It was Camus's contention that, grim though it was, *The Misunderstanding* suggested a perspective beyond itself.

If a man wants to be recognized, he must simply say who he is. If he is silent or lies, he will die alone, and everything around him will be condemned to disaster. But if he speaks the truth, he will die undoubtedly, but after having helped others and himself to live.

[26]

Like *Caligula*, *The Misunderstanding* is concerned with the passion for an absolute, with human happiness as an absolute in a human world that engenders crime upon crime. The question raised takes us full circle back to *The Stranger* and the unanswered enigma of Meursault's relation to an act he seems not to be troubled about, though he is ready to accept its consequences. In the plays no fatality is involved. The burden of disaster rests squarely on the decisions of the protagonists. All that outer circumstances offer is blind chance, and it was also blind chance, symbolized by the chain of incidents that led him to the beach, that triggered Meursault's gun. Camus, in his short novel, seems to have wanted to describe "a man," to say "who he is." His hero experiences the full range of a man's possibilities, stopping at none until, face to face with death, he grasps them in their totality: violence and compassion; beauty and death; solidarity and solitude. He is a man, that is, a "stranger"—unique, impossible, and real. Caligula discovers the violence and rejects the beauty and compassion; Martha knows the infinite nostalgia and rejects the present possibilities; Jan believes in innocence and ignores the horror. The hero in each play has only one fragment of the total awareness to which Meursault eventually accedes. Hence the conflict, the mutilation, and self-destruction that make these men tragic figures in Camus's eyes.

Underlying all three works is the same pervasive feeling of moral distress in a human society that can no longer reach outside itself for a coherent system of ethical values. The *hubris* that sets off the infernal machine of fate is thus bred in the stubborn decisions of distraught human minds. Camus insisted, with some measure of reason, that although they expressed mental conflicts or attitudes, his plays did not involve an abstract philosophy. *The Myth of Sisyphus*, which developed in the same years, and which he defined as a personal testimony, intellectualizes the mood that gave substance to his first fictional works.

The "absurd"—a word that was to hypnotize Camus's readers and critics, somewhat to his distress—seems to have begun to fascinate Camus in the summer of 1938, when both *Caligula* and *The Stranger* were under way. He was not the first to use it. The word was in the air, a part of the restless, anxious, mood of the time. It was used in a wide variety of contexts to designate the incomprehensible, the unpredictable, the purposeless, incongruous, "impossible" aspects of life. For Camus, as for Sartre, although not to the same extent, the basic mood had been conceptualized through contact with existential and phenomenological approaches to philosophy. Analysis of the failure of the intellect to encompass the complex reality of human existence was common to Pascal, Kierkegaard, and Nietzsche; to Husserl, Jaspers, and Heidegger. Unlike Sartre, though, Camus, when he wrote the *Myth*, was not concerned with a "philosophy of the absurd," but rather, given the sense of the absurd, with how profitably to live with it, transforming it into a positive incentive "to live lucidly and to create." The heavy abstract superstructure that has been imposed by critics on his short essay has tended to obscure its essential feature, its lyrical emphasis on the exhilarating reality of a life that transcends the intellect. Life is incomprehensible to be sure, but in young Camus's eyes its existence is not open to question.

The Myth of Sisyphus is a clarification of the problem of "the absurd," valid only within a given mental framework of reference and experience, Camus's own. It is addressed to those who have no religious, metaphysical, or philosophical system of belief to which they can relate their acts, and whose acts thereby lose their relevancy. Intellectual indifference and moral irresponsibility, Camus observed, are the price they tend to pay for a freedom that takes the form of an infinite array of equally irrelevant decisions; living tends, then, to become a senseless mechanism pervaded by a paralyzing sense of its nothingness. Without reaching outside this nihilism, one of the essential elements in the problem he had set himself, Camus proposed in his essay to "find a means to go beyond it."

"The fundamental subject of *The Myth of Sisyphus* is this: it is legitimate and necessary to wonder whether life has a meaning; therefore it is legitimate to meet the problem of suicide face to face." From this classical problem, Camus rapidly moved to the equally classical situation in which, in an apparently stable social world, the question of meaning arises, and with it metaphysical anxiety with regard to the whole of existence. Camus briefly enumerated the "walls" that bring rational answers to a halt, then turned to the existential philosophers, only to reject them all for the same reason. Having faced the fundamental relativity of all rational systems of explanation in a nonrational world these philosophers, Camus charges, "make a leap"; they arbitrarily and irrationally derive from the nonrational a principle of explanation.

Camus's purpose was different, different too from that of Sartre, who from the same vision of man's moral freedom and consequent responsibility in a purposeless universe, drew his terrifying ethic of a perpetual and anguished creation of the self. According to Camus, the basic limitations of human living cannot be changed, nor the contradictions resolved. If once the mechanism of routine living is stopped, if the shot rings out on the beach and awareness starts, we shall always find the same human creature in the same role: judge, accuser, witness, advocate, accused, a "Stranger," whose being remains incomprehensible.

In the first section of the essay *The Myth of Sisyphus* the age-old paradoxes are briefly summarized: the love of life, the inevitable death; the need for coherence, the basic incomprehensibility; the surge toward happiness, the evidence of pain. Camus proposes the lucid acceptance of the situation: to love life, and to live with the knowledge that life is incomprehensible; to multiply all the chances for happiness, knowing its impossibility; to explore the infinite possibilities of life within the narrow limits of a life. That the full reality of experience transcends the intellect was, he felt, an insufficient statement; he defined man's metaphysical existence by the refusal of human reason to accept definition in terms of the irrational.

The Myth of Sisyphus proposes to seek in this paradoxical and inescapable situation the source of man's unique and peculiar value, his creativity. To the destructive transgressors —Caligula, Jan, and Maria—it opposes a gallery of truly "absurd" heroes: the actor, don Juan, the conqueror, the creative artist, and finally, subsuming them all, Sisyphus. Camus's Sisyphus is man wedded to his limitations, living out the role assigned him, each conflicting part of which is integral and must be lucidly confronted.

With *Sisyphus*, the cycle of the absurd can be seen as a whole. Meursault, Caligula, Jan, Martha, and Sisyphus are all objectified, intensely personal projections of certain inner moods. The four works are related by the resurgence of recognizable images, concrete and at the same time symbolic: light, the light that suffuses Meursault's Algiers, but also an inner light, whether the cruel light of evidence, the burning light of violence, the quiet light of beauty, the soft light of acquiescence; sea, stone, and desert; human faces that appear, merge, and become autonomous beings observable by others— judge, jury, or horrified witnesses. It is not by chance that the "creator" is one of the four "absurd men." It is clear that for Camus, in the thirties, artistic creation was not a solution to a situation that he had diagnosed as insoluble, but rather a confrontation with himself, a way of existing in harmony with himself. The aesthetic urge was already so strong in him that it freed him from the Marxist dogma of "social realism," although in *The Stranger* and *Caligula*, young Camus's antagonism to established society, its institutions and representatives, so clear in his first journalistic writings, comes through in the grotesque satirical lampooning, in the novel, of the court of justice and its clownlike functionaries; and of the patricians, in the play.

In comparison, the murderous actions of a Caligula or a Martha are so violent an expression of revolt against the limitations of reality that one cannot but see in them a deeper anguish and protest whose only check was the creative act itself.

Between the years Camus conceived this first set of works and the years they were published, momentous events had transformed the climate of France. The thirties had been years of social problems, political discussions, ideological battles. Camus had taken a stand on all these; yet his creative works rose as a block, beyond them. His heroes, conscious of the contingency of their existence, all invent an "impossible" existence, based on the full expansion of one part only of the self. At the time they were created they stood outside the main stream of literary preoccupations. In the forties, they reached a disconcerted audience living in a Caligula-like world of insecurity. It was the "absurd" view of man's situation, inherent in the structure, character, and action of Camus's fictional works, that struck his readers. The underlying protest, the ambivalence of the whole, the upsurge of vital force, and the imaginative power that defined the aesthetic unity of the work tended to pass unnoticed. Artist though he was, Camus was disguised as a philosopher. But the foundations of his work were laid. Its basic language, forms, conflicts, and themes were not to vary greatly.

One of the preoccupations of Camus, clearly evidenced in his first essays, was a tragic sense of human suffering—as, for example, in Caligula's downfall. His first works, concentrating on the discovery and creation of the self, side-step the theme. The war was to bring Camus face to face with the problem. He had not eluded the question in his personal life, but it had not been an essential source of inner tension, hence of creativity. A Marxist first, then a non-Marxist socialist, he had, it seems, settled the question in his mind. War and occupation, liberation, and the political no man's land of postwar Europe imposed on Camus new concepts involving the relation of the artist to the human community. The basic theme underlying the second, "Promethean," cycle of Camus's work is the conflict between an obsessive, collective situation involving large-scale injustice, mass murder, enslavement, and torture, and a no less obsessive longing for the freedom to breathe and to create a harmonious work of art. In his articles and speeches, throughout this period, he dwells on the inroads political action makes on an artist's creative powers.

Opposed to Sartre's theory of political commitment, as well as to the Marxist view of the artist, he defined solidarity with the oppressed as one of the sources of the artist's integrity. The artist could not, in certain circumstances, not militate. In the political arena for better or worse, he could not, however, change his language in the interests of a party. He could not let his writing serve in dubious ways, for this would betray his art, corrupting his use of language itself.

How deeply Camus felt the disruptive pull of these two factors in his life during the fifties, his speeches and works illustrate. To be free from the harrowing obsession with horror and the petty disputes of politics, to write as he wished, was the nostalgic aspiration of these years. *The Plague, The Just Assassins,* and *The Rebel* constitute a statement and a working out of this conflict. The counter-myths Camus created, incarnating the force of his reaction to the concrete, oppressive world around him, express his claim to something other.

A first version of *The Plague* was finished in 1943. The Plague, as symbol, had appeared early in Camus's personal imagery, perhaps first striking his attention in a strange essay, "The Theater and the Plague," written by a former surrealist, Antonin Artaud. The symbol is already at work in *Caligula* —Caligula is the plague—and up to its last appearance, in *State of Siege*, it was to prowl in the background of Camus's imagination as the most representative of the calamities that can befall a human society. In 1941 he jotted down a title for a novel: "The Plague or Adventure." It was no longer a question of describing a subjective metaphysical Caligula-like adventure. The plague, by then, had taken on a specific form, so eloquent that retrospectively it was to give *Caligula* and *The Misunderstanding* levels of meaning Camus had not anticipated. With these topical meanings the new novel originated. "The Plague," Camus wrote a friend, "that I wanted to be read at several levels, has nonetheless as its evident content the struggle of the European resistance against Nazism."

For several years Camus read extensively, plunging into the vast literature extant on the scourge—memoirs, chronicles, treatises, and works of fiction—Boccaccio, Kleist, Pushkin, Manzoni, Defoe, and the Bible. In the course of the writing, the novel changed. The fragments of a first draft are charged with savage irony.

But by 1943, irony had given way to a bleak and desperate seriousness. Camus was in France, ill and ever more deeply involved in the struggle against the occupants. He could measure the ruthlessness of the machinery of oppression grinding millions of human beings to death. The plague, which he had

[33]

first cast in the guise of a grotesque, outrageous bureaucrat, now became a killer, invisible but all-pervasive, regulating, tabulating, insulating, dehumanizing, silencing. For quite a while Camus searched for a mode and tone for his narrative that would transmit the atmosphere he wanted. A first-person narrative, centering interest in one individual, would not give a sense of the collective nature of the "adventure." Camus did not want the narrator to become an epic hero; a completely objective recording would lack the immediacy of testimony—the narrator had to be "one of us." The solution was suggested to him by the opening chapter of Dostoevski's *The Possessed*. The chronicle of the plague is written by a citizen of Oran who in the last pages gives his reasons for undertaking the task and so reveals his identity. His social position is functional; he is a doctor. He writes for several reasons: "So that he should not be one of those who hold their peace, but should bear witness in favor of those plague-stricken people"; secondly, "to state quite simply what we learn in a time of pestilence: that there are more things to admire in men than to despise"; and thirdly, because

he knew that the tale he had to tell could not be one of final victory. It could only be the record of what had to be done, and what assuredly would have to be done again in the never-ending fight against terror and its onslaughts, despite their personal afflictions, by all who, while unable to be saints, but refusing to bow to pestilence, strive their utmost to be healers.

Rieux knows that the plague bacillus never dies and that the day would come when "it would raise up its rats again and send them to die in a happy city."

Critics have objected both to the symbol Camus chose and to the mode of narration, more on realistic or even political grounds than on aesthetic ones. For the socially "committed," the plague as an invisible evil, abstracted from human beings—

the Nazis—smacked of "bourgeois idealism," of a conscience "situated outside history," of the refusal politically to accept the "dirty hands" involved in action. For others, the symbol itself—its appearance and development, the closing-off of the quarantined city—seemed too far removed from actual medical process, too obsolete to be credible. The deceptiveness of the third-person chronicle, and the carefully controlled, factual, "descriptive-diagnostic" tone, seemed to others to circumscribe too rigorously the effectiveness of the book, while the combination of symbol and testimony in the eyes of some turned the novel too obviously into an allegory.

Camus had answered these objections for himself. He had carefully chosen his terrain: the atmosphere of collective suffering; the inner tensions; the gradual snuffing out of individual aspirations; the sense of impotence and frustration. He was dealing with a struggle in which he had proved his own capacity for action, recording rather the price paid in the process. It was not the black and white, the right and wrong world of war, political parties, and their ethics that he wanted to describe and endorse; heroic postures seemed to him irrelevant and inappropriate in the impersonal atmosphere of modern warfare.

Against the terrifying description of the rise, rule, and decline of the plague, what he threw into the balance may seem flimsy: the stubborn, weary, unglamorous struggle of a few men; the deep joy of a night swim outside the pestilence-ridden city. A confession, Camus said, but also the creation of a counterimage to liberate him from the grip of his experience —perhaps, too, to tunnel a way out for others as deeply oppressed as himself. To the great plumes of smoke rising from the collective funeral pyres responds the inner flame of comradeship in the service of human survival that marks the limits of the plague's dehumanizing power.

[35]

The Plague develops at an even tempo, relentlessly, in five parts, each concerned with a certain phase in an overall movement. The narrator first evokes an everyday existence that the plague, remorseless and compelling, transforms into a fantastic, visionary hell. Each phase in the investment of the city has as countertheme the muffled orchestration of human voices exchanging views, attempting to elucidate a position with regard to the unthinkable reality. Rieux, Tarrou, Rambert, Grand, Paneloux, and Cottard propose variations of the human answer to the plague, as persistent as the whistling of the scourge over the sun-baked city. What explains, perhaps, the impact of this most widely read of Camus's works, despite the critics, is the eerie blend of stark realism and poetic vision that characterizes it. A gloomy but courageous book, *The Plague* was an effort at detachment from the tangle of historical and sociological interpretation, so that the reader could be made aware of the affective impact of the experience on the behavior of a social group, and of the appalling power of revelation of the scourge itself.

State of Siege, a play Camus wrote in collaboration with Barrault, who staged it, is a kind of exuberant final exorcism. Camus attempted to give it an epic quality, using a medley of music, mime, and dance. Unsuccessful, so far, at least in performance, the play expresses the great burst of joy and hope that came with the Liberation. How widely the hope and exaltation were shared by other intellectuals, Simone de Beauvoir's *Memoirs* show. *The Just Assassins* and *The Rebel* now completed an itinerary that had led Camus gradually to counterbalance the constricting demands for public commitments by a new affirmation of a *joie de vivre* as the source, which he could no longer deny, of hope and creativity.

In much the same way as *The Myth of Sisyphus* had posed the problem of suicide in order to conclude with a "lucid invitation to live and to create," *The Rebel* posed the question of "logical," "legalized," ideologically justified murder in order to conclude with an act of faith in the value of free, affirmative, individual creativity, in the present and "beyond nihilism." But in the politically charged atmosphere of literary Paris in the early fifties, the book had unforeseen, and viewed from the outside, inexplicable repercussions. The violence of the militant Communist press is hard to take seriously. *The Rebel* was denounced as an "ignoble" book whose purpose it was to "justify anti-Communist repression, anti-Soviet war and the assassination of the leaders of the proletariat." In the ever more "committed" *Temps modernes*, Sartre's periodical, Camus was soundly taken to task by one of Sartre's then close friends, Francis Jeanson, sparking a bitter dispute such as periodically shakes the French literary world. Clearly Camus had touched on a burning issue. Yet he claimed that in an impersonal form, his essay was a personal exploration of the implications of tendencies apparent in an intellectual climate which he carefully situated in postwar Europe. He presented it as an attempt to clarify his own position in order, "the world being what it is, to know how to live in it." It would be idle to summarize the movement of the essay, entirely directed toward the exposure of the paradox whereby revolt in the name of freedom and justice, a generous, creative, and Promethean impulse, flounders and collapses in police states, Prometheus ending inevitably as Caesar. Whatever the shortcomings of Camus's documentation and point of view, the fact remains that there was not one of his opponents who did not see in the essay a direct attack on Stalinist Russia and the reduction of the Marxist credo to a gigantic myth. This no doubt was the case, but only within the framework of one of Camus's persistent themes, the equivocal dynamism whereby, in the human mind, aspirations are rationalized into logical impera-

[37]

tives, then used as justification for a machinery of action that brooks no opposition, a catastrophic dialectic. With *The Rebel*, Camus was merely carrying this view into the realm of political ideology and action. The more specific criticism of the Marxist "leap," its consequent justification of the means by a hypothetical end, disguised as inevitable, predictable, and concrete—though it could hardly be missed—was a secondary, not a primary objective.

The Just Assassins, produced in 1949, had created no such stir, yet the themes and conflicts of the play are organically linked to the essay. In those years, justice in relation to politics was a live issue. For Camus it was a disturbing issue that the liberation and the Stalinist repression in Russia had posed in all its ambiguity. Once again he used the theater to explore the problem—to illuminate it from within.

An austere play, *The Just Assassins* borrows its cast and external design from the history of a small terrorist group who in 1905 had assassinated the Grand Duke Sergei, Russian Minister of Justice. Camus unified the action by dramatizing the internal conflicts and tragic repercussions the assassination itself seems to have created in the tightly knit group of terrorists, concentrating on the tragic awareness of the two idealistic central figures, Kalayiev, the thrower of the bomb, and Dora, in love with him. The play, begun in a climate of eager heroism, ends in a disturbing atmosphere of ambiguity and doubt. It has no thesis; it merely shows the irreconcilable disparity between the generous initial impulse, its ideological justification, and the suffering endured by the flesh-and-blood people involved in an act like Kalayiev's. Kalayiev and Dora confront the tragic paradox of their action in its unforeseen personal consequence, the mutilation of their lives. "Scrupulous murderers" in Camus's eyes, they reach the extreme limit of the permissible. The play, again, is a counterimage set up in protest against the "complacent" bureaucratic murderers righteously and safely engaged in mass repressions justified by an implacable faith in an ideology.

More deeply than *The Rebel*, *The Just Assassins* underscores the basic theme of the Promethean cycle: the extreme predicament of the artist faced with extreme injustice. What Kalayiev and Dora eventually lose is their flesh-and-blood vitality, the richness of their sensuous relation to the world, to one another. It is the poet who dies, and with him Dora's power to love. With the creation of Kalayiev, Camus was laying aside the heroic romanticism of the war, freeing himself from the obsession with political responsibility that had been characteristic of the Resistance years. The secret, inner itinerary he had been following can be traced in the eight lyrical essays written between 1939 and 1953 that he collected under the title *Summer*. They revolve around a few central images woven into the fabric of his language: the sea, the desert, the "immense African nights," the "black buried sun" burning at the heart of the artist's work. Thematically the essays show an ever more persistent emphasis on beauty, happiness, art; light as opposed to darkness, night as opposed to black despair; the great sweep and freedom of the sea as opposed to the closed prisons of men expressing an increasingly confident joy in life, qualifying the somber atmosphere of the Promethean cycle. That the artist, committed to freedom, cannot serve the political designs of those who "make" history was by now Camus's firm conviction. He had come to terms with the problem of "commitment"; he was definitely committed to the difficult path of individual integrity, free from doctrinaire imperatives. But before he moved to more personal concerns, Camus fired a parting shot as wildly disruptive as Meursault's revolver shot on the beach. With *The Fall* he unleashed the most histrionic, equivocal, and sardonic of creatures, Jean-

[39]

Baptiste Clamence, self-appointed "judge-penitent," a "hero of our time," and any conscious man's double.

Jean-Baptiste Clamence is not an individual but a voice, reminiscent of the demon who spoke with Ivan Karamazov and the one who reveled in Job's torment. *The Fall* is a short novel in the form of an impassioned monologue or "implied dialogue," such as that used by Dostoevski in his *Notes from the Underground* and James Hogg in *Private Memoirs and Confessions of a Justified Sinner*. The speaker is a seedy lawyer, who encounters his silent interlocutor in a bar in Holland. Clamence's inspired rhetoric, disguised as a confession, spirals around his interlocutor, apparently at random. But it has design and derives its momentum from a secret, fixed, inner purpose. The patterning of the disconnected facts Clamence reveals in his specious confession gives *The Fall* the appearance of an irrefutable demonstration, but one whose conclusion is always elided. Clamence's fall, or so he insinuates, is linked to a leap that he failed to make, a leap over a bridge to save a slim girl in black.

A perfect individual, according to the generally accepted nineteenth-century bourgeois ideal, Clamence, one night hearing laughter that rings sardonically behind him, discovers the delights of self-questioning, anxiety, and then guilt. So he runs the full gamut of twentieth-century consciousness, eagerly examining his most ordinary gestures, carrying ever further the distintegration of his formerly "noble image" of himself. Vanity, insincerity, and eroticism finally lead through a variety of sins to sacrilege. And all lead back to one reiterated proposition: Self-knowledge leads to the contempt of self, and of all men. Carefully selecting his data, Clamence repeatedly follows through to the brink of this indictment and stops, leaving it to the interlocutor to leap, to admit that there is only one remedy to personal perversity—the abdication of freedom.

Clamence, fully enjoying his shame, will never leap, the St. John the Baptist of an anti-enlightenment.

The diversity of interpretations proposed for *The Fall* underscores its ambiguity. It has been read as an admission of guilt on Camus's part, as a retraction of his former statements, more particularly in *The Stranger*. Yet the satiric, diabolical figure of Clamence hardly seems to warrant so flat a reading. As we leave the judge-penitent, shivering with fever on his bed, in solitary tête-à-tête with a stolen painting, "The Just Judges," a panel of Van Eyck's "Adoration of the Lamb," we would be hard put to it to think of him as a "straight" character. A virtuoso with words, and a consummate actor, aggressive, fawning, sure of his ultimate mastery, Jean-Baptiste Clamence is in truth the inspired perpetrator of a colossal fraud; and he is also a man frustrated, shut in upon himself, who cannot break the charmed circle of his isolation. The caricature of the artist as Camus conceived him, a caricature and a perversion, Clamence reveals at last his basic impulse toward self-destruction. Clamence, Camus indicated, is an "aggregate of the vices of our time," and Camus has fused them all into his hero's fraudulently disguised project.

Perhaps, as it has been suggested, Camus was expulsing Clamence from himself, or attempting to counter the image of himself as a "good man." But these seem banal and very partial explanations. There is something gleefully Swiftian about *The Fall* that savors of vengeance. The battle of *The Rebel* was not far distant, nor the bitter polemics with Sartre. Even the writing and method of exposition in *The Fall* take on the semblance of the Sartrean dialectic. And there are closer connections. In 1952, Sartre had published his extensive psychoanalysis of Jean Genet, *Saint Genet, Actor and Martyr*. "Actor and Martyr"—the words fit Jean-Baptiste Clamence perfectly. A thief and jailbird, and a writer to boot, Genet,

Sartre suggested, is a kind of scapegoat, virtually thrown out of the city walls with the secret evils of society magically heaped upon him, a thoroughly Sartrean interpretation. He became thereby, in Sartre's eye, "one of the heroes of our time," in fact an image and symbol of what we are fated to be, denizens of an impotent society, incapable of "the leap" that would put us on the right side of history. Clamence's hollow voice seems curiously to echo Sartre's, as Camus leaves him in his rhetorically built "cell of little ease," on the brink of a leap he will never take, free to accumulate a sterile guilt with which he inoculates others.

Whatever the "figure in the carpet," *The Fall* revealed new potentialities, perhaps even to Camus himself. A short novel like *The Stranger*, it had originally been designed as one of a series of short stories that Camus had begun to work on.

The six short stories of *Exile and the Kingdom* present considerable variety in theme and form, from the quasi-naturalism of "The Host" to the elusive symbolism of "The Growing Stone," and the allegorical suggestiveness of "The Renegade." In each story a situation is carefully delineated in concrete terms and presented with apparently complete objectivity and great attention to plausibility. The situations are potentially dramatic, except in "The Artist at Work" and "The Renegade," and they build up to a crucial moment of decision, free and open in its possibility. An insight is reached, experienced, and acted upon—though not verbalized. The resolution turns on a simple impulse, a movement toward greater understanding that casts an aura of nobility on the quite ordinary protagonists. The impulse that "goes wrong," eventually ending in disaster, so fundamental a theme of Camus's previous work, fashions only "The Renegade," a monologue and lament, closely related to *The Fall*.

"The Artist at Work," in contrast, is an ironic variation on the theme of the artist as scapegoat. The painter Jonas, a public figure besieged on all sides by obligations, finally takes refuge in a hideout, where one day he collapses, leaving a single unfinished word scrawled across his empty canvas. Whether solitude or solidarity, who can tell? Somewhere between these two conflicting exigencies, the modern artist has to find his equilibrium. The story is an ironic commentary on one of the most crucial problems of Camus's own existence, one that was operative even in his death.

After *Exile and the Kingdom* one more work only is crucial —the stage adaptation of Dostoevski's *Possessed*, a novel that had deeply impressed itself on Camus's imagination when he read it as a youth. Dostoevski's restless cast of men driven by a passion for destruction—"possessed"—are the very embodiment of the enemy Camus had been fighting—which Dostoevski had defined as "the spirit of negation and death" in all its forms and varieties, from the most frivolous to the most insidious, compounded in the mysterious figure of Stavroghin, on whose secret crime, evolution, and fate Camus centered his play. Moving from "satirical comedy, to drama, to tragedy," Camus's adaptation sets up as a counterimage to the "dead souls" of the nihilists, the poignancy of human love, manifest in Chatov, the victim of a senseless murder. *The Possessed* is a synthesis, a grand orchestration of Camus's previous work, a kind of leave-taking.

Camus's work shows a marked inner coherence and unity. He is not a wide-ranging writer, drawing his power rather from deliberate self-limitation. Like most of his contemporaries, he gave much thought to the relationships between art and the specific circumstances, social and historical, in which he found himself, and to what might truly characterize the

[43]

modern consciousness. He thereby touched upon some of the crucial issues of the period—in politics, philosophy, and religion.

In his own daily living, in the decisions he made and the actions he carried out, he attempted to achieve and maintain some kind of balance between thought and act, a difficult enterprise which he considered with a rather wry and ironic stoicism. In public affairs he is heir to the reasoned though qualified optimism of the Enlightenment, opposed to any fanatical cult, whether of the rational or irrational. He was an advocate of "dialogue," of the open mind and the scrupulous act. He shared with the existentialist philosophers the sense of the contingency of human life and the gratuitous nature of human aspirations and values. But he accepted the situation as fundamental, man as present with his characteristics and limitations. The "absurd" and "revolt" are the two terms he chose for expressing the insoluble paradox of the human situation as he saw it. It was not his purpose to conclude, expound, or dictate, but to live and to write. He was not, he claimed, a philosopher, but an artist. His essays merely define the self-chosen limits of his art. In his 1954 preface to the reissue of his first book of essays, *L'Envers et l'endroit*, he compared the artist's career to a tightrope walker's performance, a traditional image, which illustrates the aesthetic urge to achieve an apparently harmonious equilibrium by a hard-won control over conflicting forces. Some of the disruptive forces at work in mid-century were ostensibly social; but there were, too, personal disruptive impulses in Camus's own personality that furnished the more fundamental substance for his art: the Meursault-like urge to give free reign to the sensuous enjoyment of life, indifferent to the rest; and the equally strong urge to achieve a Caligula-like nihilism in lucidity. To keep both impulses in check, without plunging into one extreme or the other, Camus needed his

[44]

art. His often repeated statement that he could not live without it is not merely rhetorical. It also explains each work's ambiguity. Camus is never absent from his work nor is he on one side or the other in the conflicts he describes; he is affiliated with all his characters, examines and recognizes them all. But only with *Exile and the Kingdom* does he seem to have replaced the ultimate criticism and rejection of his "impossible" characters by the creation of "possible" and acceptable ones. Camus's rejection of extremes, in an age given to excesses, is a powerful factor of originality.

His work clearly belongs to one of the main currents of modern Western literature, which he himself has designated by his references to Melville, Dostoevski, Proust, and Kafka. For these writers, the external patterns of the narrative, concrete and specific, lead to a central inner meaning, which initially organized them. Camus's narratives and plays combine a surface simplicity and apparent realism with a consistent design. The titles he gives his works, some of which have Biblical echoes, all have a concealed relation to the theme developed. Camus's intent, like those of the writers to whom he refers, is, through fiction and by means of situations and characters, carefully delineated, to illuminate an aspect of experience, an illumination that is *experienced* within the narrative, and not demonstrated. The integrity of the work and its force of conviction depended, Camus felt, on the artist's effort to "sacrifice" nothing. Hence, Camus's power to reach his readers even when such concepts as "the absurd" and "revolt" seem unpersuasive.

What characterizes his own techniques as a writer is formal control, a natural consequence of his preference for the Greek ideal of beauty, an effect too of his fierce drive for coherence. The clarity of outline, the sharpness and precision of the details observed, the overall effect of detached objectivity, trans-

[45]

mit a sense of formality, even of constraint, that runs counter to the more powerful trends in contemporary art. The human content and significance run counter to others, more abstract.

The recurrence of images, figures, themes, and patterns, within each work and from one work to another; the rhetorical texture of the language, its range of tempo and rhythm—these give Camus's writing an enigmatic intensity, in direct relation to the restraint he imposed on his expression. The limitations inherent in this combination of clarity and controlled design very much concerned Camus. He wanted to overcome them, envisaging for the future a greater freedom of expression. But he belongs to the tradition of conscious thinking and hard discipline in art. His control of his medium, coupled with his conception of art as the illumination of an individual experience, communicated and universalized, sometimes pushed his work to the border of parable. Wherever the tension in the quality of Camus's writing slackens, and rigor of thought shades off into truism, or emotion into pathos, a certain moralism tends to overshadow the deeper underlying theme. This occurs more particularly in the works of the Promethean cycle, which deal with conflicts less deeply rooted in Camus's own complex personality, and in fact hostile to what he felt impelled to say. Camus had defined his own realm quite early and explored it with sustained intellectual and artistic integrity, thus achieving a difficult balance between the erotic and the critical, between the solitude of the self and the claims of society. There are, of course, other works, other expressions just as valid as his, but his writing seems to have the decisive resonance that we associate with durable works of literature.

SELECTED BIBLIOGRAPHY

NOTE: *No attempt has been made here to list the numerous prefaces, essays, articles, and translations by Camus. Indeed, only the major works of and about Camus are included. Albert Camus's complete works have been published by Imprimerie nationale Sauret in six volumes (I: Récits et romans; II: Essais littéraires; III: Essais philosophiques; IV: Essais politiques; V: Théâtre; VI: Adaptations et traductions), in 1961 and 1962. Volume I (General Edition) of Oeuvres complètes, edited by Roger Quilliot, and published in 1962 by Gallimard, has also appeared (Théâtre, récits, nouvelles). Paperback editions of American translations of many of Camus's works have been published in the Vintage series.*

PRINCIPAL WORKS OF ALBERT CAMUS

La Révolte dans les Asturies. Alger, Charlot, 1936.

L'Envers et l'endroit. Alger, Charlot, 1937.

Noces. Alger, Charlot, 1938.

L'Etranger. Paris, Gallimard, 1942. (The Stranger. Tr. Stuart Gilbert. New York, Knopf, 1946; Vintage, 1954.)

Le Mythe de Sisyphe. Paris, Gallimard, 1943. (The Myth of Sisyphus. Tr. Justin O'Brien. New York, Knopf, 1955. With other essays: Vintage, 1960.)

Le Malentendu *suivi de* Caligula. Paris, Gallimard, 1944. (Caligula *and* Cross-purpose. Tr. Stuart Gilbert. Norfolk, Conn., New Directions, 1948. Caligula and Three Other Plays. Tr. Stuart Gilbert. Preface by Camus, translated by Justin O'Brien. New York, Knopf, 1958. The latter includes L'Etat de siège and Les Justes.)

Lettres à un ami allemand. Paris, Gallimard, 1945.

La Peste. Paris, Gallimard, 1947. (The Plague. Tr. Stuart Gilbert. New York, Knopf, 1948.)

L'Etat de siège. Paris, Gallimard, 1948.

Les Justes. Paris, Gallimard, 1950.

Actuelles: I (Chroniques 1944-1948); II (Chroniques 1948-1953); III (Chroniques algériennes 1939-1958). Paris, Gallimard, 1950, 1953, 1958. (Resistance, Rebellion and Death. Tr. Justin O'Brien. New York, Knopf, 1961.)

L'Homme révolté. Paris, Gallimard, 1951. (The Rebel. Tr. Anthony Bower. Preface by Sir Herbert Read. New York, Knopf, 1954; Vintage, 1956.)

L'Eté. Paris, Gallimard, 1954.

La Chute. Paris, Gallimard, 1956. (The Fall. Tr. Justin O'Brien. New York, Knopf, 1957.)

"The Artist in Prison." Tr. Antonia White. *Encounter*, No. 6 (March, 1956), pp. 23–29.

Requiem pour une nonne (a play adapted from Faulkner's novel). Paris, Gallimard, 1957.

L'Exil et le royaume. Paris, Gallimard, 1957. (Exile and the Kingdom. Tr. Justin O'Brien. New York, Knopf, 1958.)

Réflexions sur la peine capitale. Arthur Koestler and Albert Camus. Paris, Calmann-Lévy, 1957.

Discours de Suède *et* L'Artiste et son temps. Paris, Gallimard, 1958.

Speech of Acceptance upon the Award of the Nobel Prize for Literature. Tr. Justin O'Brien. New York, Knopf, 1958; *The Atlantic*, CCI, 5 (May, 1958), 33–34.

Les Possédés (a play adapted from Dostoevski's novel). Paris, Gallimard, 1959. (The Possessed. Tr. Justin O'Brien. New York, Knopf, 1960.)

Carnets. mars 1935–février 1942. Paris, Gallimard, 1962. (The Notebooks. 1935–1942. Vol. I. Tr. Philip Thody. New York, Knopf, 1963.)

CRITICAL WORKS AND COMMENTARY

Brée, Germaine. Camus. New Brunswick, N.J., Rutgers University Press, 1959. Rev. ed., 1961.

——, ed. Camus: A Collection of Critical Essays. Englewood Cliffs, N.J., Prentice-Hall, 1962.

Cruickshank, J. Albert Camus and the Literature of Revolt. London, Oxford University Press, 1959. Paperback edition, including a tribute to Camus, New York, Galaxy, 1960.

Hanna, Thomas. The Thought and Art of Albert Camus. Chicago, Regnery, 1958. Paperback edition, Gateway, 1959.

Maquet, Albert. Albert Camus: The Invincible Summer. Tr. Herma Brissault. New York, Braziller, 1958.

Sartre, Jean-Paul. Literary and Philosophical Essays. Tr. Annette Michelson. New York, Criterion, 1955.

Spector, P. D. "Albert Camus, 1913–1960—A Final Interview," *Venture*, III, 4 (Spring–Summer, 1960).

Thody, Philip. Albert Camus: A Study of His Work. New York, Macmillan, 1957. Paperback edition, Evergreen, 1959. (Revised, 1961.)

Bei Fragen zur Produktsicherheit wenden Sie sich bitte an:
If you have any questions regarding product safety,
please contact:

Walter de Gruyter GmbH
Genthiner Straße 13
10785 Berlin
productsafety@degruyterbrill.com